Small Acts of Kindness

by James Vollbracht

illustrated by

Christopher Fay

Paulist Press

New York/Mahwah, NJ

Library of Congress Cataloging-in-Publication Data

Vollbracht, James R., 1950–
    Small acts of kindness / by James Vollbracht ; illustrated by Christopher Fay.
      p. cm.
    Summary: Illustrates the power of kindness, showing how one small act can have unexpected effects.
    ISBN 0-8091-6629-1
    1. Kindness—Religious aspects—Christianity—Juvenile literature.
[1. Kindness. 2. Christian life.]   I. Fay, Christopher L., ill.
II. Title.
BV4647.K5V65   1995
241'.4—dc20
                                     95-36334
                                         CIP
                                         AC

Published by Paulist Press
997 Macarthur Boulevard
Mahwah, New Jersey 07430

Printed and bound in the
United States of America

*O*ne morning, a little boy
gave his mother a big hug—
for no reason at all!

This so pleased his mother
that she made her husband's
favorite breakfast.

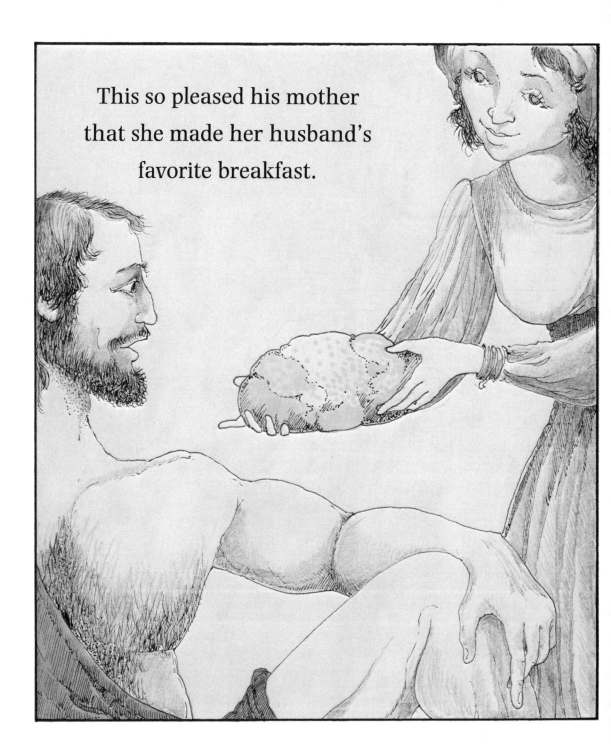

Her husband felt so warm and happy
that he carried a heavy load
of wood over to the widow
who lived next door.

The widow was so delighted
someone had thought of her,
she finished knitting a scarf
and gave it to a passing soldier.

The soldier was so surprised to receive a gift, that when he arrived at the river's edge, he carried a woman on his horse across the swift river.

The woman was so grateful for the ride, that she helped the country girls hang their freshly washed quilts in the early afternoon sun.

The country girls were so pleased to have their chore finished early, that on their way home, they offered a cup of cool water to a beggar who was sitting beside the road.

The beggar
was so refreshed,
that he dusted off his old
wooden flute,

and played a beautiful melody
that echoed across
the countryside.

The farmer, who was
driving his oxen to the village,
was so enchanted by the music,

that he helped the wheel-smith
pull a cart out of the mud.

The wheel-smith was so appreciative for the help, that he cleaned the mud off the merchant's cart for no extra charge!

The merchant, who was used to paying for everything, was so pleasantly surprised,

that when he saw a young
shepherd boy sitting alone
alongside the road,
he stopped and gave him
a bottle of precious oil.

The shepherd boy looked up at him
gratefully, knowing just what
he would do with this gift.

Truly, it is the
small acts of kindness
given freely
along the way

that become the
greatest gifts of love!